10637732

me and Nina

WITHDRAWN

No longer the property of the
Boston Public Library.
Sale of this material benefits the Library.

WITHDRAWN

me and Nina

POEMS BY
MONICA A. HAND

ALICE JAMES BOOKS
FARMINGTON, MAINE

© 2012 by Monica A. Hand
All rights reserved
Printed in the United States

10 9 8 7 6 5 4 3 2 1

Alice James Books are published by Alice James Poetry Cooperative, Inc.,
an affiliate of the University of Maine at Farmington.

ALICE JAMES BOOKS
238 MAIN STREET
FARMINGTON, ME 04938

www.alicejamesbooks.org

Library of Congress Cataloging-in-Publication Data

Hand, Monica A.
    Me and Nina : poems / Monica A. Hand.
    p. cm.
    Includes bibliographical references and index.
  ISBN 978-1-882295-90-6 (alk. paper)
    I. Title.
    PS3608.A69924M4 2012
    811'.6--dc22
                            2011015817

Alice James Books gratefully acknowledges support from individual donors, private foundations,
the University of Maine at Farmington and the National Endowment for the Arts. ❦

Cover art: Krista Franklin

Contents

Acknowledgments

My sincere thanks to the editors of these publications for first publishing the following poems:

Aunt Chloe: A Journal of Artful Candor: "Libation" (as "Call her name")

Beltway Poetry Quarterly: "*Everything Must Change*"

Black Renaissance Noire: "Regret and Pride speak," "The Need to Be Touched speaks," "The Gray Sky speaks"

Boog City: "Jim Crow"

Bop, Strut and Dance: "Daddy Bop"

Connotation Press: An Online Artifact: "From the Language of Ash," "Things That Stink," "The Spirituals speak"

Days I Moved Through Ordinary Sounds: The Teachers of WritersCorps in Poetry and Prose: "Upward Bound" (as "Bound")

Generations: "dear Nina (I am Venus Hottentots)"

Lily. A Monthly Online Literary Review: "Zuihitsu on the Lover Who *It Might as Well Be Spring*"

Naugatuck River Review: "Black is Beautiful," "Black People Sure Can Keep Secrets," "A Red Box For," *"How it Feels to Be Free,"* "Snuff," and "Colored"

Radius: "Some Sign of Nature," "Freedom speaks," "dear Nina (When Lucille died)"

The Sow's Ear Poetry Review: "Worry Beads"

TORCH: poetry & prose by African American Women: "The Curtis Institute speaks," and "~~Eunice Waymon~~"

In loving memory of Monte Elliott Hand and Christine Althea Hand

It is the duty of the living to heal the ancestors
and by so doing you will heal yourself . . .

—Malidoma Patrice Somé

Sound speaks

traveling through us she found rage
inside our breath a seaquake
simple mathematics: ear + voice = reverberation
we implode one into the other
she to us like geese migrating
like a locomotive like a wagon like land claimed with a rake
like a psalm
we in her presence
the Jubilee

Regret and Pride speak

We found her when her fat legs still dangled

We knew what she was
Men and fools would kneel before her
Wallow in their spit and semen for her favors
Use her hurt her to hide their shame

Before she could even talk
We had her. It was undignified unkind greedy

No good for her to taste the drink
So close to the tit
No good to render intoxication
Before she'd held the joystick

How could she explain the knowing she was different
How could she hold the knowing

What would you do if your feet felt like weights
pulling you to a floor you could not reach

Keep your back straight is all she knew

The Need to Be Touched speaks

My baby beat me but he didn't mean to
My baby beat me he don't mean to
Call me a fool it may be true

Take a blue pencil to my memories
Blue-pencil my memories
Line out all the black and blue

I tried to be on my own but it was no good
No good on my own I was no good
Tell you the truth my body's no fool

What difference does it make
Gentle sharp the marks love make
Something you can feel

Something I can feel
Is all

Colored

for Aunt Sarah, Safonia, Sweet Thang, Peaches, Black Bird, Darkie, Midnight, Mud, Pass for White, Cream, Pinkie, Sandy, Honey, Pearl, and Red Bone

dear Nina

When I was a little girl
they'd sit me in the sun
white bonnet

Vaseline skin
bare rear
for a good tanning

why don't you have
black friends
I'd ask my daughter

my mother's father
looked like a white man
beat us with his cane

when my father struck

his big black hands
her yellow cheeks
colored red

9

my sister was born
with freckles
skin the color of milk

my father said
who you been fucking, bitch

my African lover hates me
when I call myself black
he calls me white

because he's darker

in winter when I'm pale
my son says I must be
mixed with white

Everything Must Change

Rufus is taking me to the Blue Note to see Nina Simone. I try to hold back my excitement so I don't jinx it. Like the time Aunt Ermine was going to take us skiing. Or that time daddy said he would visit.

Rufus is late but still takes time to butter up my mom: *Your home is so lovely. Don't worry, I'll take good care of your daughter.*

His smile is big and juicy like a stick of chewing gum. He bounces on his feet when he walks and is never still. He is so skinny and black. The blackest boy in the neighborhood. My mother and I are red-bones. And he can talk. A sweet talker like my daddy.

No sooner then we leave my house Rufus says he has to make a quick stop. He doesn't have to explain. I know what he wants to do. Not many boys ask me out and the promise of seeing Nina Simone holds my tongue.

I wait outside while he does his business.

Don't be mad, he says when he comes out. *That man robbed me now I have to go back home to get some more money.*

Once we are inside his room in the basement of his parent's house he starts begging me to give him some—*just a little* he says. I've never done it before and I'm not scared just not really interested. I want to go. See Nina Simone. He begs real hard. Even gets down on his knees like James Brown: *Please, please, please.* I give in. Stop his begging. It's over. Quick. No big deal. I don't feel a thing.

We never make it to see Nina Simone.

I don't see much of Rufus after that. And when my mother asks what happened to him I just shrug my shoulders or tell her I think he's dead. Just like, I tell the kids at school who ask where's my daddy.

Daddy Bop

Knew him like a fifth of vodka
he tasted good with sugar and lime
—left me with the shakes
so if you see me on the street
acting like a bitch—
I'm just missing my daddy

early in the morning, I heard the call of the crow

He beat my momma stayed out late
slept with other women
up and down the block even went
for the bull dagger's femme
till she beat him with his bottle
might find me too
in a bottle

If you ever come looking for me

early in the morning, I heard the call of the crow

Lost all my self-respect
in bed with some men some women
who smelled like my daddy
if they could love me, maybe he would too
just understand everybody needs
some respect he was my daddy

Some truth some lies I'm telling you
Some truth some lies I'm telling you

early in the morning, I heard the call of the crow

The Curtis Institute speaks

She just wasn't good enough
Didn't stick to the score improvised
We train classical musicians

We heard jungle music in her score
This is the Curtis Institute not church
She just wasn't good enough

She had a great talent—sure
Only the best get in Curtis
We train classical musicians

Bach, Chopin, Beethoven nothing more
Each of them played with brilliance
She just wasn't good enough

No genius – unrefined, primitive
Not up to our standards not prepared
We train classical musicians

She was too dark too blue
Made us feel unsure impure
We train classical musicians
She just wasn't

Upward Bound

Me and D we are in Upward Bound, a summer program just for us city kids who are college bound. English, math, history, science. But it's mostly about us. Black people. Not Negroes—Black People. Our teachers are college students home from school for the summer. They talk about Revolution about change. They are Black and they are proud. They teach us how to move our feet. We journalize, write poetry, draw and film our neighborhoods, stage Lorraine Hansberry's *To Be Young Gifted and Black*. Each flat nose girl is Nina Simone singing from her gut—angry then sad then proud. They say it is the new Black National Anthem. Me and D we are college bound upward bound. I write a poem about living in the projects even though I really live in a three-family house on Ninth Avenue. D makes a pretty dashiki from a Vogue pattern. We are young gifted and Black. And we are proud.

Mrs. Massinovitch

my little colored girl
classical born musician
you'll shake this world

turn it like a Ferris wheel
my little Eunice Waymon
my own little colored girl

I'll send you off to school
with a very special fund
leave behind this world

its poor time gospel
its Holy Roller tunes
be free little colored girl

understand me now
play all over town
won't get you my world

we may spin under your spell
but we won't be re-born
can't un-color this world
colored girl

My grand baby says she is a princess
Even though she lost months ago
Or broke all the parts to the costume
Plastic crown pendant rings
I sing her a bedtime song too dark and deep
For lullaby a monster's double vision
Inside a baby Cyclops noise

Zuihitsu on the Lover Who *It Might as Well Be Spring*

What is the order of things undone?
The thread unravels into a pile on the floor.
Beautiful installation: thread into a mountain into a mountain of dust
a mountain of

Bleu et gris et blanc

Every season you conjure my feet

After sex we pretzel
no salt no mustard just stickiness before we are drunk
you want me to put you in my mouth you lie under me very still it is your way
you talk marriage
children with someone else some other continent some other universe
you know I've already had these things

I get up from the bed your smell for now enough

Sew from the bottom up each signature tight inside before the next fold inside
and outside use a bone folder an even number of signatures press each signature
before sewing the next follow the thread be careful not to pull against the grain
don't be afraid to undo the thread

Sewing with cross-stitch bikini cut keloid seams

Be careful of a man who smiles all the time   mother's proverb

You hardly do and when you

Love me love me say you do let me fly away with you for my love is like the wind wild
is the wind   sings Nina

Daddy a would a could a should a gonna man like you
But I should never think of spring cause that would surely break my heart in two

Black People Sure Can Keep Secrets

We sure can. We sure can keep secrets. Secrets that won't go away no matter how good we keep them. I learned today my friend's daddy's been touching her. She comes to school all edgy wanting to fight everybody even me. Now you don't understand my friend is not the type to fight. She's nice always smiling or singing. I like her around. We don't talk that much really. Mostly we just listen to music. Nina Simone is our favorite. My friend is quiet. So am I. Guess I understand why she don't tell. But why she don't tell me don't she know I can keep secrets. She told my mother. My mother tells me. My friend thinks if I know I will tell. I want to tell her I already know. But my mother says we have to keep it a secret. I know how to keep secrets. My mother doesn't know I know her secrets too. I hear her. I hear them. I hear late. I keep the dark.

Snuff

kill slay assassinate execute put to death slaughter massacre waste

Sunday mornings before church my grandfather would feed us soft-boiled eggs in porcelain cups insist we get down on our knees and pray he'd bluster and spit his praise beg forgiveness for our unclean selves our weak ways my nana quietly moved in the background mute witness when she died from an explosion in her brain my mother took her place sneaking us paper napkins for the boiled eggs pillows for our knees

ground or pulverized tobacco applied to the gums rather than inhaled

Nana roamed the kitchen like a ghost making biscuits and frying chicken fresh from the icebox chickens she had fed and tended chased in the yard before she wrung their necks and then quietly watched them run headless until they tired and died they said she was part Indian I would watch her dip snuff from a yellow box kept in her apron pocket pinkie fingers her dipping sticks she'd mash the snuff in the space inside her bottom lip which made her face look like a horn player blow fish or bad embalming then she'd spew the tobacco juice onto the big black coal stove used for cooking the sizzle her spit made

dear Nina

I am Venus Hottentots
my brain
my cunt
in a bell jar
my skin plastic alabaster
painted brown
my teeth cow bone
my black buttocks
carnival display
sold high sold low
my dirty sex
my strange sex
monstrous
music video
newsstand thong
a blue nude
a secret
only my sisters know
the bustle dress
the bustle chair
can't imitate me
I refuse to uncover
my apron
tell them
I am human
tell them
to turn away their gaze

~~Eunice Waymon~~

my name an omen
my name sin

my name
my name a moan

Nina
Nina Simone

dear Nina

I want vengeance
an eye for an eye
a dish served cold
two wrongs
a tale of two cities
contrapasso
ill will
a settling

not with a grain of salt
with a heavy hand

a slow burn
boiling point
a huff and a puff
blow the mother-fucking house down

no cage forestalls
no age forgets
no gene forgives

I cane those who give me
this fury

a hundred lashes
acrimony and dander
needle and tizzy
umbrage
ruckus

Freedom speaks

I am

    a. what you say
    b. sold like gold, ivory, spices, skins, precious stones
    c. on auction block, with shackle lock, whip and chains
    d. butler, cook, mammy, maid
    e. all of the above
    f. none of the above

Rank in order of importance

    ___ bomb, pyre, petrified flames
    ___ four little dead girls in ponytails
    ___ scarred tongue, combustion-tongue, no tongue

Fill in the blanks

Somali pirates	on the open sea
Gangsta rappers	love
Blacks on Wall Street	don't
Clarence Thomas	give
Langston Hughes	a damn

Multiple choice (circle one)

    a. no hands, no feet

    b. blink, cataracts

    c. transformation by the renewing of the mind

    d. good fuck, okay fuck

    e. none of the above

    f. all of the above

Sounds like

    a. riot

    b. belly laugh, side split, thigh slap

    c. joke, gag, jest, jape

    d. debauchery, revelry, bacchanal ritual

    e. none of the above

    f. all of the above

Some Sign of Nature

That day on the laundry bench outside, an escape
from heat of dryers people folding; that day
the homeless man from the park nearby out his mind
out half his clothes can't chase me back inside
where people spin and washers moan; that day I see
two baby birds burrow their beaks in cracks
they want for food, unearth crumbs the absent-
minded drop as they rush away; that day
at the Long Island Railroad station every seat taken
by someone down on her luck waiting
as police sweep through with their sticks, demand
those sitting show their tickets or leave –
the woman next to me gets up, men from the back
where it's dark, leave; a woman with the wrong
ticket leaves – mad, pushing her bags
someone with the right ticket has to stay awake
that day he overlooks me – just my luck;
in the news, pictures – smiling pundits, the famous
poems read on the subway – bear, wolf
that day I walk aside half starving trees

dear Nina

      my daughter called today
says she will sleep in her car
I make my heart rock
it won't break
her baby says nothing
counts fake coins spills
some all

Nina my daughter called from West Virginia
                    years ago to keep out of jail
                    the only black girl in the car
today
she says she's done won't talk about it
won't go back to the hospital
not drinking
taking her meds
just doesn't feel good
doesn't want to be here
not in West Virginia
not anywhere

What do I do, Nina?
I have no way to get her home

Nina she's at the river with no phone
calling me on her ex's line
tells me leave well enough alone
I spell out all the bad parts
so her baby won't hear
so baby don't hear

Sonnets for Unrequited Love

2

words from the book I am reading
a slow day in the rain

song off shuffle
hopeless as a penny with a hole in it

a long way to go from here
here to
too many here

from the book words repeating
rain slow summer day in my my my

can I call you that?

a hole in
hopeless

daze

4

metronome
(of desire)
horn car alarm
my head
tied to a tree
I would have a wife
who has not lived as a girl
a girl who is a woman
a woman who was a girl
leaking
natty girl
her body ruptured seams
molten unsound
hostage

7

I will not ask you back
to my jewel box

leave me these
stones

wet to spit
spit
spit

act like you don't know
like your day ain't needing
thinking of me

just so
you got smack
plenty

plenty

dear Nina

my daughter texts:

ur screwing me
really fucking bad
really fucking bad

ur getting my phone calls
u know that I know
i hope you know

i could have screwed u
just like u screwed me
ur wrong u no it too

thanks a lot u hear me
i have nothing
i hope u get nothing too

Confessions of John Divine Waymon

for Eunice

I was good with my hands—a handy man. I built things, cut hair.
    I broke things too.

I promised her we would be free.

I could skin a hog.

I knew she was special. (I never told her.)

My son was a cripple. A hole rotted my stomach.

I loved her naturally. A father's love.

She was my beloved.

I never claimed to be God.

Each house got smaller. Such is the kingdom of God.

I promised her she would be free. (She never forgave me.)

I couldn't go to her.

I couldn't go to her.

Alone, Naturally

after Bhanu Kapil

Who is responsible?

        for the suffering of the mother

father: you are

                       I knew you'd be dying soon

sister called
says you are dead

        I realize
        I despise you who
        I once called
        father

Your word
dust

                    blind
                    still
                    searching

violin
unstrung

already
a ghost

Your wormwood
shell

       all

                   my life
                   broken

tiny welts that
sing

                   'til death do
                   us part

what a woman says
when she thinks
children aren't
listening

I want you to die

                  three weeks for you *to die*
                  three weeks for you *to die*

a lifetime for you to die

every night   you're

      calling

me

I won't go
to your bed

to your
dead body

      you're
      my broken heart

Holy Ghost

      Leaving me to doubt
      God in his mercy

If you really do exist
father

Nina Looks Inside

Sometimes Nina I'm tired of listening to you
Tired of being so blue tired of these lonely times
Don't want to listen to you
You make me feel

All the love I could beg steal or borrow
Is just a great big empty bowl
Tired of paying these dues

Nina what are we going to do
What we going to do

Can't stand these blues
Don't want anything else to do with you
Don't know what else to do

Nina I'm tired of listening to you
I get so hot why is it so hard why has so little changed
I'm tired of you reminding me

I don't want to hear it no more
What makes you so cold why can't you go
Where the chilly winds don't blow

I'm tired of your complaining

Tired of this crazy mad
Tired of you reminding me

What we still don't have

Nina
I'm sick and tired of listening to you
Don't like your every song
I'm *tired of* your *moods*   *this* arrangement

Tired of the same old tune
Want a different rhyme a different kind of melody

Don't want to hear about no suffering
Don't want to crumble and break
I need a different kind of heartache

Sick and tired of this
weeping willow tree

Nina I can't listen to you no more   everything you say
takes me   away

 I hope
The time will come

takes me far from here not to Mississippi not to Alabama not to Georgia
not to the post office

I'm tired of listening – every season

your every good-bye song

going nowhere

Nina I
in my chest   a mosquito   a wasp
a bass guitar spending

drum beat metronome
high tone places

one note

Libation

Soul singer
Harp singer
Harpy
Wailer
Town crier
Drum speaker
Dirge chanter
Wood thrush
Redbreast
Call her name
Blues singer
Face down
Blue bottle
Bluecoat
Shift blue
Blue tongue
Bluenose
Blue water
Blue sky
Call her name
Jazz singer
Unleashed
Unnamed
Ash

Folk Singer
Ordinary
Dirt Clay
Ground
Call her name
Gift from God
Left hand
Right hand
Straight
Round
Owl
Snail
Lion
Roar
Raw
Wool
Refuge
Call her name
Revolt
Revolver
Rewake
Received
Satellite
Orbit

Call her name
Revive
Carol
Chant
Chirp
Hum
Warble
On the down
beat
The complex
Screech
Trumpet
Poet
Call her name
Crooner
Soft slide
Half lit
Heirloom
Yahya
Lumumba
Oya
Baubo
Baubo
dancing

Sow
Gorgon
Witch
Zigzag
Zip gun
Coolness
Call her name
Cinnamon
Tree
Tree frog
Tree snake
Tree root
Shade
Bed
Water
Eunice
Niña
Nina
Nina
Harpy
Wailer
Town crier
Drum speaker
Dirge chanter

X is for Xenophobia

like the *x*
in a geometry problem or hex
I don't understand their pain
why they act like chickens in a pen
as if they felt at their nape
broken bone
why they want me alone hobo
for preaching hope
for reminding people we are Ibo
not bane
cause of soullessness they took an ax
to my happiness I want to open
the door play classical piano
now my hipbone
slips to Obeah
I am the unanswered z y x

Bach Fugue speaks

I changed
like at the revival meeting
when the evangelist laid her hands
on that crippled boy and he ran like a fugitive
or that stuttering crazy bitch started talking polyphonic
shit
real sense not gibberish
I was made
pure
commotion
certainly verily amen
my keys shattered
teeth
she inside me
my God

Resistance

no rest

until the last Pullman porter leaves the train
until we are near

Miriam, Odetta, Lorraine told me *Nina* be certain
take a stance don't just sit

hold them in a trance
sear

no pusher man no segregation   art

my weapon my voice my song arsenic
don't expect me to be nice

I will make a scene
stir it up set

carts

you cannot erase
me
or my race

The grand baby asks if I'm happy
Each time I say *I am* she asks, why?
I say *because you are with me*
All the while my heart is open
Spilling into the streets on the train
In the grocery store on these white pages

From the Language of Ash

The translator undresses. Tries on the shape of the work she translates. Stuffs her new belly with his engorged sex. Tries not to re-write his words tries to give her self over to his syntax. In the end, she wears her same nakedness.

volcano spews ash
thick clouds that touch the heavens
cover her body

transient—passing by or away from one place to another.

her thick fingers
trees damaged by a hard storm
downed power lines

rendering something written or spoken in different but equivalent form or state to a different place, office, or sphere by which information in messenger RNA directs the sequence

from the language of ash: *the women in her family are beautiful and alone.*

yellow park flower
its petals its leaves
brown

Black is Beautiful

Me and D in our crushed-velvet jackets blue-jeans high heels. We are going to New York City to see Nina Simone at the Apollo. We're taking the path train across the river then the subway uptown. D knows her way around. She goes to FIT. I've been to the Apollo many times before but this is the first time on my own. Just me and D. We are going to see Nina Simone. At the Apollo. Our seats are way up in the balcony. The orchestra section is full of white people. Nina is singing *Mississippi Goddam*. Me and D we look at each other and nod. Nina plays the piano a long time as if she forgets we are there. But we are. Nina goes Holy Roller African all in one wave of her hands ragtime to classical and back again. We are in her groove our seats rocking with our bodies. Our young female bodies, big Afros and big dreams. The balcony is a smoky black sway. The orchestra white. Someone fidgets. Another one coughs. Nina stops. *Quiet.* Her voice a swift typhoon. You could hear their hearts hesitate. Stop. Nina chuckles then returns to her song. *Mississippi Goddam*. It's different now. Bruised. Me and D we look at each other and nod. We are at the Apollo. It's Nina Simone.

Daughters

Some daughters always hurt
forever the six-week old clutching your art
the cry you hear
when you leave every hard
day for work the unforgiving bob head
hidden in every storybook you have read
of make-believe mothers who tear
their bodies loosen earth
who never settle a baby's rage
two souls in a duet
one sings of missing hugs
the other her declining age
who could defend argue
for pretty poems when flowers gather
around your feet catch you in the hunter's rude
snare who will stand guard
who is the thug
who ravishes chokes on the dregs
disenchantment buried in every myth heard
of an ill-fated mother's tar
baby story forgive me dear daughter

Things That Stink

Drunks
their breath their sweat
especially when they are lying on top of you
or when they have fallen off of you and you are listening
    to them snore and fart
when they are your father stumbling up the stairs or passed out
    on the sofa
in all his clothes smelling of cigarettes vomit and stale women's cologne
when he is smacking your mother around and you can smell her near
you are supposed to be sleeping
when they sit next to you on the subway
when they yell "hey baby" as you are walking to school
when they are happy dancing with their pants falling off
slobbering on your neck playing cards talking shit
just mean

when they are lilies at a funeral

bed sheets the day after when the dark has removed its mask

My grand baby says she's sad
Because she lost her mommy
Again and again and again
She wants to tell me a story
She says her mommy
Hurt
The poem she knows

The Spirituals speak

With their many tongues, we were the one language
    they could each speak
Even the *masters* understood underneath hump and hale,
    labor of the load
We healed the numbing made

Even when she abandoned us for the music of bars and sex,
    you could hear
Spirit in her sway, watch her feet remember stomping
Her body ring shouts

We made her we un-troubled the waters became her balm in Gilead
A deep down light in her darkest days we a band of angels
Come to take her home

This morning she flies from room to room
A butterfly with purple wings; she woof woofs
Cock-a-doodle doos, meows and growls
Dance with me she says until I get up
We waltz and two-step she dips and spins
She laughs and laughs until I am laughing too
The sun is up she says and celebrating

How it Feels to Be Free

me Nina and Gil fly in unison
Float like a tunnel
k-i-s-s-i-n-g over the yard
mooning the guards
smoking some good dope

go farther than sky
almost got lost
this time
found ground
in a piece of sunshine

I go to social services
they treat me like a criminal
take my picture my fingerprints
president is a black man
make no difference

Go to Marcus Garvey Park
Play for the drum
Drop the hopscotch
two steps forward
three steps back

me Nina and Gil
we gonna get over this time
we not lose our mind
cause we know how it feels
(how it feels to be free)

me at social services
mad as a hungry yard cat
yes sir no ma'am with a slur
mad babies mad mommas
mad work mad cops for hire
drunks crazies jambalaya

me at social services line by line
in a room full of split peas
me don't want to hurt nobody
at the border
at social services
on line hold on
hold on

A Red Box For

Miss Nina I
have a box a
red box a box
of missing things
keep my red box
in the morning
early early
fore the sun crows
a red box for
missing things touch
them care for them
put in what I
find save come by
like today it
was the short side
of a wishbone
fountain pen ink
a river map
a needle thread
swallow feather
the turned pages
of a Bible
twenty-third Psalm
tomorrow hopes
I find something
You Miss Nina
don't you worry

Patches of Black Snow

She loves snow. I love her chubby little hands. She laughs. I love her laugh.
When she throws snow at me. Small clumps never really balls. Small patches of
snow she steals from the roots of trees. Small patches of snow just outside the
apartment door where in the summer weeds grow. Sooty snow. Walked on snow.
It's been almost a year.

Almost a year since. Almost a year since

Late at night I sit by the window. Patches of snow darken the streets.
Magical deer appear.   Bengal tigers without stripes.

The Gray Sky speaks

The smell of erasure
The earth stretching to re*live*
To be remembered in fragments

In Octavia Butler's "Wild Seed"
She can grow back her limbs
That's what we need

The brokenhearted, the alone
The sticky sound of the heart
Beating

Worry Beads

He looks like a man who would worry who would cause worry
not count beads one by one with a prayer anger radiates
from his body or is that my body that hums I don't look at him
I know to humble myself in the presence of such fervor
dust on his clothes face hands a familiar ash
I imagine him a construction site in line with other men
he waits not to be chosen I imagine him a wife
who no longer loves but feels his obligation
children who wish he never had but feel his need
I imagine his fists his feet his fumes his hot face
him grabbing my throat his eyes drills hammers
I imagine him a string of beads that breaks

Jim Crow

I will not cow
before you

I will not row
my boat out to meet you

I will not crow
your coming

you in the balcony black as bitter crow

tell Jim
tell Jim

we aint scared no mor
we aint scared of him no mor

tell Jim
tell Jim

we are to the cor
impenetrable

tell Jim
tell Jim

he had better watch out for my mo
jo

Alma Thomas speaks with Nina and Lorraine

I am not abstract   I am   expression

global
           in the Whitney
the Corcoran

in defiance   of their

             segregation   We are the same

We refuse   marginalization

We do not extract   ourselves

black is

authentic   enough   our lines innovation

Nina you say: *to stay out of any category*
freedom

your voice doesn't need to sound like a woman
Lorraine – wear pants   if you desire

My oblique shapes and muted colors
Pirate Jenny Sydney Bernstein's window

                                      in our hands

                  the color line on fire

Movement for Three

There are many things in life we don't understand,
but we go on anyway.

—John Coltrane

Nina:
Music is black
black classical music

Jimi:
Excuse me while I kiss the sky
Music is a safe kind of high

Nina:
Once I understood Bach
I understood me

They ask me what's *free*
It's just a feeling: No fear

Jimi:
I'm free because
I'm always running

Poet:
The sweet release
into vocabulary

dear Nina

She tells me that the slave cabins
are still there . . . and the graves of the slaves
are there, unmarked. The graves of my family.
—Lucille Clifton

When Lucille died, it was as if I heard God's voice
—I suddenly knew what I was missing

Not like the woman across from me on the subway
—missing her front teeth

Or the homeless man with his scary voice
—missing the threat of a loaded gun

Lucille knew where she come from she comes
from Dahomey women, women with one breast

The women I am from are wild; beautiful
This is what I know

When Lucille died, I tell my grand daughter
We are like Lucille trouble in the water can't kill us

Strong Man

Bob: Why they say one not use the herb?
           Everybody dies Nina.
           The herb is a plant
           See God
           It make you rebel.

Poet: I knew a man, African
           We drank lots of wine
           red wine and Heineken

Bob: Many more will have to suffer
           many more will have to die
           don't ask me why.

Nina: If I need the solitude
           as I often do
           I will go to any church
           But I don't need to
           music is my God.

Poet: Women keep leaving me
           for God.

           Why do they prefer God to me?

Nina: All around me all over me
my mind weaves dreams.

Poet: I am afraid of everything
especially God

dear Nina

I am not a thief
I am not a kettle
or an undress

I am not a fly
piece of meat
or kitchen sink

cold beer
picnic chicken
empty noose

I am not recession
depression
oppression
compression
crooked line
broken line
polka-dot
parking lot
or spot

I am a *Gift from God*
I know

I am

a contrapuntal
song

Fodder in the Wings

all I have ever wanted
is
to be
the full span of her wings
my wings

why did God give us wings
give us wings

clip our wrists
then say fly

wing load so heavy

won't pull me down
under dirt

my wings my wings

fodder in my wings
dust in my brain

can't close the sky

So I'm Gonna Leave You the Blues

Langston:
Keep working until they open up the door
When they open that door
Make sure you tell them where to go

Nina:
One day I thought I could fly
I look down at the sea
No me   no hands no feet

Poet:
Gonna act up
Shake the blues
'til they shake me back

Bandog (Chained Dog) speaks

doggo dod doggo dod doggo dod doggo dod doggo dod god nag gag beg nag gag beg bane bend bone bang band bond doggo dod doggo dod doggone dang odd ode goad bode doggo dod god dog god gone one dod doggo dod dod dead dod doggo dod doggo dod doggo dod doggo dod doggo dod nag gag beg nag gag beg bane bend bone bang band bond doggo dod doggo dod doggone dang odd ode goad bode doggo dod god dog god gone dod doggo dod dod dead dog doggo dod doggo dod doggo dod doggo dod doggo dod god nag gag beg nag gag beg bane bend bone bang band bond doggo dod doggo dod doggone dang odd ode goad bode doggo dod god dog god gone one dod doggo dod dod dead dog doggo dod doggo dod doggo dod doggo dod doggo dod god god god god god

bone bang band bond doggo dod doggo dod doggone dang odd ode goad bode doggo dod god gone doggo dod doggo dod doggo dod doggo dod doggo dod god nag gag beg nag gag beg bane bend bone bang band bond doggo dod doggo dod doggone dang odd ode goad bode doggo dod god dog god gone one dod doggo dod dod dead dod doggo dod doggo dod doggo dod doggo dod doggo dod nag gag beg nag gag beg bane bend bone bang band bond doggo dod doggo dod doggone dang odd ode goad bode doggo dod god dog god gone one dod doggo dod dod dead dog doggo dod doggo dod doggo dod doggo dod doggo dod nag gag beg nag gag beg bane bend bone bang band bond doggo dod doggo dod doggone dang odd ode goad bode doggo dod god dog god gone dod doggo dod dod dead dog doggo dod doggo dod doggo dod doggo dod doggo dod nag gag beg nag gag beg bane bend bone bang band bond doggo dod doggo dod doggone dang odd ode goad bode god

gone one dod doggo dod dod dead dog doggo dod doggo dod doggo dod doggo dod doggo dod nag gag beg nag gag beg bane bend bone bang band bond doggo dod doggo dod doggone dang dod doggo dod doggone dang odd ode goad bode

Notes

Several poems in this collection contain anagrams of the titles in most if not all of the lines:

> "Bandog (Chained Dog) speaks" [bondage, bandage]
> "Daughters"
> "~~Eunice Waymon~~"
> "Jim Crow"
> "Resistance"
> "X is for Xenophobia"

In 1941, Nina Simone was eight-years old and began taking classical piano lessons with Mrs. Muriel Massinovitch until 1947. In some biographies, "Massinovitch" is spelled as "Mazzanovich."

After graduating from Julliard, Nina Simone applied to the most prestigious classical piano training school at the time called the Curtis Institute. She was not accepted. This rejection radically altered the course of Nina Simone's life and career.

The name "Gil" in "*How it Feels to Be Free*" refers to Gil Scott-Heron, "Langston" in "So I'm Gonna Leave You the Blues" is Langston Hughes, "Jimi" in "Movement for Three" is Jimi Hendrix, and "Bob" in "Strong Man" is Bob Marley.

Lyrics and samples in the "Daddy Bop" are taken from Gil Scott-Heron's "Delta Man" and "The Bottle."

Titles of the poems *"Everything Must Change," "How it Feels to Be Free,"* and *"Alone, Naturally"* come from the names of songs Nina Simone is famous for singing.

"Sonnets for Unrequited Love" samples *Hopeless* recorded by Dionne Farris on the *Love Jones* soundtrack.

"dear Nina" (*I am Venus Hottentots)* was inspired by the conference "Hottentot Venus" as well as the anthology *Black Venus 2010: They Called her "Hottentot"* edited by Deborah Willis.

Recent Titles from Alice James Books

Alice James Books has been publishing poetry since 1973
and remains one of the few presses in the country that is run collectively.
The cooperative selects manuscripts for publication primarily
through regional and national annual competitions. Authors who win a
Kinereth Gensler Award become active members of the cooperative
board and participate in the editorial decisions of the press. The press, which
historically has placed an emphasis on publishing women poets, was named for
Alice James, sister of William and Henry, whose fine
journal and gift for writing went unrecognized during her lifetime.

Typeset and Designed by
Pamela A. Consolazio

Printed by Thomson-Shore
on 30% postconsumer recycled paper
processed chlorine-free